AND THEN CAME
HOPE

AND THEN CAME
HOPE

*Reflections on a Journey
toward the Light*

Joan Brown

SunrisePress
Lakeway, Texas

SunrisePress
212 Capri
Lakeway, Texas 78734

Email: publisher@andthencamehope.com
Website: www.andthencamehope.com

Cover image by Jerry Brown
Cover and book design by Sheila Setter

Manufactured in the United States of America.

ISBN 978-0-692-58691-4

Dedicated to a wonderful man
who has been a huge blessing to me
for the past fifty-five years,
a gift from God,
my husband Jerry.

❧ ◆ ☙

CONTENTS

INTRODUCTION

By Jackie Leonard

I first became aware of Joan Brown in early 2000. I was sitting in daily Mass with a friend, Marge Lutz, and sitting a few pews ahead of us was a woman wearing a black velvet slouchy hat. Marge told me the woman had stage IV melanoma on the top of her head, and the prognosis was poor. Marge had found the slouchy hat at a thrift shop and given it to Joan to cover the wound on her head. Knowing Joan as I do now, I'm sure she hated that hat. It was too black, too velvety, and too slouchy. But she wore it because Marge had given it to her.

After Mass, I met Joan for the first time and was totally floored. Instead of being frightened, she was serene. Instead of anger, she radiated peace. I saw nothing but kindness and calmness. I was mesmerized. How could this be? How could this woman facing a cruel death be so smiley, so peaceful, so serene? Her attitude fascinated me.

I converted to Catholicism in 1984, mainly to close the family circle. During those sixteen years before meeting Joan, I advanced in my faith, growing slowly closer to God; and of course, I met many men and women who were deeply faithful to Him. However, Joan was different. Despite being so very sick, she was joyful...as joyful as she was sick.

I wanted that joy.

One day in Bible study, our leader asked what we wanted from the Church. I said I wanted the peace, serenity, and joy that come only from God, and I was convinced those gifts only come from fully trusting Him.

The woman beside me looked at me and said, "You want to be Joan Brown."

YES! Yes, I did...well, I didn't want to *be* Joan, but I did want the kind of trust that she has found!

ॐ ◆ ೞ

None of our misfortune in life comes from God, however much He allows us to suffer.

Joan taught me that.

All you can do is pray. Really.

Another lesson learned from Joan.

I've been so blessed to have Joan in my life as a dear friend and mentor. I feel so blessed when I take Jesus to her and share the Eucharist with this wonderful woman. And then we share laughter and joy and hopes and fears. God is good.

ಬಂ ◆ ೞ

After reading Joan's book, I was struck anew by the life experiences that shaped this wonderful woman. We can all relate to the ordinary events that bring hurt into our lives. Joan explains how to respond to the hurts—or "stones" as she calls them—that are thrown at us. She helps us understand that, with grace, we can react with love, without judging others, without hurting them when they hurt us. She shows us how to face adversity simply by trusting our God and loving Him.

So many of us have broken parents, face serious illness, harbor deep-seated fears. Joan has faced down all of these and more. She has done it lovingly, with the grace that has been gifted to her—and grace is available to each of us if we only ask for it because God is good.

Fɪʀsᴛ ʟɪɢʜᴛ

Recently, a twenty-eight-year-old woman gave me a heartwarming compliment. "You are not like most old people," she said. "You think young."

Yes, I *do* think young. Why is this?

I think it is because I have learned the secret to a happy and peaceful life.

"*And what is that?*" you may ask.

TO LIVE IN THE PRESENT MOMENT

I know what you are thinking: *Easy for you to say!*

No, it wasn't always so easy; but when I began living in the present moment, two wonderful things happened. First, I no longer dwelled on the past. I stopped counting my years, and I stopped feeling old. And because I couldn't anticipate the future (and worrying about it won't change what happens anyway), it became easier for me to get up each morning and just enjoy the day. It became possible—even while experiencing serious illness—to appreciate the gift of each sunrise. And oh, how lovely and full of promise a sunrise is when each tree, each flower, each person that greets it is etched in the day's first light.

How was I so fortunate to arrive at this peace and contentment, this ability to live in the present moment?

First, I had to deal with the past and let go of it.

This can be very difficult, especially when we have had bad experiences, and everyone has something in their past that they think is unpleasant or downright awful.

I understand this.

There was a time when holding on to my past kept me tied up in unforgiveness and misery; this allowed other people and situations to control me. It affected how I lived—and let me tell you; I lived in this darkness for half of my life.

But one day, the darkness fell away, and it was followed by a light so beautiful, so overwhelming that darkness has not overtaken me again. Now each of my days starts with a beautiful sunrise; and even on those days when dark clouds float through, the joy permeating my life cannot be diminished.

> *Yesterday is history,*
> *tomorrow is a mystery,*
> *today is a gift from God,*
> *which is why we call it the present.*
>
> ~ BIL KEANE

Do I sound like Pollyanna? That's surely not my intention. I want you to experience the joy I have been blessed with.

How do you achieve this?

Well, you may not wish to read the following statement; but if you continue, you will discover for yourself what I have discovered:

> *To experience the true joy of being*
> *in the present moment, all we need do is*
> *walk with Jesus.*

You may say to yourself, *He does not walk with me,* or *I do not believe in God,* or express some similar sentiment, but the truth is we do not know God by feelings or earthly wisdom. We know Him by witnessing His grace. If you are open to God's grace, you will experience Him in every step of your life.

And if you accept His love and reciprocate it, your relationship will grow.

To truly walk with God, I had to accept the truth that He loves me, that He lives in my heart, and that He never leaves me no matter how much I push Him away. Before I understood this, I found it hard to grasp God or encounter Him. I judged Him as others treated me. When I felt betrayed or judged by others, I felt betrayed and judged by God. I didn't trust Him because I couldn't trust anyone else.

> *Ever present in your midst, I will be your God,*
> *and you will be my people.*[1]
>
> ~ LEVITICUS 26:12

For more than half my life, God lived "out there," in the universe, not close to me. And because of my perception of God, tending to my spiritual life and going to church felt like duties—obligations that I owed to God. I felt like God was constantly judging me—and I felt so alone. But through God's grace and the circumstances I experienced in my life, I gradually, gently was led to this truth: God truly loves me, UNCONDITIONALLY LOVES ME. He lives in me; He is always beside me. I can never do anything to destroy His love for me.

And when I realized and finally accepted this truth—that God lives in me—I experienced His Light. Jesus. The Light of the World.

Light is the symbol of truth.

~ JAMES RUSSELL LOWELL

Now, no matter how much stress is in my life, I am still filled with joy because I know Jesus is walking with me, holding my hand; and I have come to truly understand, "I have the strength for everything through him who empowers me" (Philippians 4:13).

If you do not understand, if you do not believe me, I challenge you to read this book and then tell me what you think.

Let me tell you my story.

· PART ONE ·

Blessed are you who are now weeping,
for you will laugh.

~ Luke 6:21 ~

৪০ ◆ ଓଃ

Chapter One

Hard Times

I was born on October 2, 1936, in Tulsa, Oklahoma. It was the middle of the Great Depression, and Tulsa was the middle of the Dust Bowl. Because life then was so different from what it is today, it may be difficult to understand what it was like living during those hard times.

The Great Depression struck the country in October 1929 when the bottom fell out of the stock market. Within two months, nearly all the banks had collapsed, average families had lost their savings, and many had lost their homes. Many more people lost jobs.

But those dark days of October were only the beginning. The Dust Bowl, as it was called, occurred during the middle of the Great Depression. Caused by improper plowing of the land and extended drought, huge amounts of soil that had once been productive farmland were picked up by windstorms and swirled around in air so thick no one could see, much less breathe. The hardest hit was Oklahoma. The Dust Bowl forced tens of thousands from their farms. Families moved, mostly to California,[2] to find work and a place to live so they could feed their families.

As the Great Depression progressed and times got tougher, young men and even teenage boys were forced to go where they could find work. Take a moment to consider the heartbreak as they left their families to take the pressure off because there would be one less mouth to feed. Perhaps they'd hear about a job in a distant town and hop a passing train, hiding in the freight car because there was no money for a ticket, only to reach their destination and be forced into another long line stretching for blocks—and all of this was done just to get work so they could feed themselves.

You've got to go out on a limb sometimes because that's where the fruit is.

~ WILL ROGERS

Most of the fourteen million people out of work during the Great Depression survived because of their deep faith in God and their will and determination. The young men and boys who left families to find work did so out of love and a willingness to do whatever necessary to make good lives for themselves and their loved ones. And despite hardships, many went on to productive lives—men like journalist Eric Sevareid, TV host Art Linkletter novelist Louis L'Amour, oil billionaire H. L. Hunt, and Supreme Court Justice William O. Douglas to name just a few.

℘ ◆ ℘

Reflection

"For I am the LORD, your God, who grasp your right hand; It is I who say to you, Do not fear, I will help you" (Isaiah 41:13).

Chapter Two

CAN WE AFFORD IT?

Like so many other men trying to provide for their families, my father lost his job when the Great Depression struck. My brother was three years old. Although things improved over the next six years, when Mother became pregnant with me, she and Dad were still not "out of the woods" financially. So it is probably no surprise that when Mother told my nine-year-old brother she was expecting, he didn't ask, "Is it a boy or a girl?" He asked, "Can we afford it?"

Can we afford it?

When Mother told me this story, it affected me for a long time. Not only because I was too young to understand how difficult it had been for them to survive during the hardships of the early 1930s, but also because I misunderstood "it."

Can we afford it?

By the time I was born, my brother was nearly ten; by then, he had heard, "Can we afford it?" many times. When he had asked this question of Mother, what he meant was, could she and Dad afford the cost of the doctor and caring for a bigger family, but my ego understood his "it" to mean "baby"…me.

As I grew up, I remember thinking to myself, *I am not an* it.

Was I a mistake? Who knows? But that was the feeling I had for most of my life.

It's possible my parents were not too excited when Mother became pregnant because they had moved in with her parents after Dad lost his job, and the only work he'd been able to find paid a dollar an hour.

How easy it is to misconstrue what others say and then feel hurt or get angry.

How habitually we carry that burden of hurt throughout our lives.

ॐ ♦ ೞ

Reflection

"In my Father's house there are many dwelling places. If there were not, would I have told you that I am going to prepare a place for you?" (John 14:2).

Chapter Three

STICKS AND STONES

I remember very little about the first three years of my life, except that I wished my Aunt Betty were my mother. Although we saw her only occasionally, Aunt Betty always made me feel special. She called me her "little doll" and showered me with unconditional love.

Mother made me feel uncomfortable—I felt like she was always judging me, and Dad was just "there." My brother was too busy with his friends to have time for me, and I don't recall having any playmates of my own. The result? A profound feeling of loneliness—a feeling that greatly affected me with a spirit of sadness for much of my childhood.

ℬ ◆ ℰ

My friend Pat frequently says we are a product of our family of origin. My father's parents divorced when he was nine. Divorce was considered terrible in 1913, but my grandmother didn't care. She went on to remarry and divorce several times, and Grandfather simply shut down.

At the age of nine, my father had a nervous breakdown. His grandmother took him in and he recovered, but then he was sent off to military school. Dad was probably never held and loved; and although he was a wonderful man with deep integrity and always physically present, he did not know how to show his love for us with hugs and kisses or affection.

My mother always acted as if she was being slighted. She fought continuously with her sisters, and her feelings were always hurt. Neither my dad nor my brother or I could ever do anything to please her. What made Mother the way she was? I believe she never felt accepted as a child, and that created deep insecurities.

Perhaps my grandmother treated my mother the same way that Mother treated me. I recall Grandmother giving me lots of attention when I was small, but that ended when I was five and my cousin was born. Then she dropped me like a hot potato; and all of her attention focused on him, as if I no longer existed. Did she treat my mother the same way?

Sticks and stones. When we get hit by them, the impact leaves a mark. Mother mentioned one time a stone that hit her as a child...and it was a very big stone. My mother was born during the flu epidemic that hit the whole country in the early 1900s. Not too long after that, her five-year-old sister died from the flu. One day, Mother heard my grandmother say to a friend, "She might have lived if I had not been so busy with the new baby."

Mother took this to mean that my grandmother blamed her for her sister's death. Mom carried this burden in her bruised heart all her life. Furthermore, Mother's two living sisters were twins; and as the grandmother of twins myself, I know how much commotion (and therefore, attention) they can require. So Mom may have felt left out because her sisters commanded so much of their mother's time. For these or whatever reasons, Mom was insecure...and so she *needed me* to be perfect and accepted by everyone. But I wasn't perfect! And all this did was make me feel very unworthy and afraid of doing anything because it might be wrong.

I don't know how my brother looked at our home life; however, my guess is he was deeply affected, too. He never wanted to talk about it, which usually means it is too painful to discuss.

ೞ ◆ ೲ

Reflection

"He will wipe every tear from their eyes, and there shall be no more death or mourning, wailing or pain, [for] the old order has passed away" (Revelation 21:4).

Chapter Four

THE FIRST STONE

My brother had a statue of Jesus in his bedroom. The statue had an open heart with Jesus's hand and index finger pointing to it. I vividly recall, at the age of three, sitting in the doorway of his room and looking at that statue because I was not allowed in his bedroom. Although I did not understand it at the time, sitting there and looking at Jesus with His open heart brought me peace and put salve on my loneliness.

ଓ ♦ ଓ

I have been hit by four big stones in my life. Each one left a bruise on my heart. These bruises greatly affected me…and for a time, I withdrew into myself. You may have had stones hit you, too. They leave painful bruises that often do not heal until we put salve on them.

There are many kinds of salve, but most simply mask our pain; and when we experience something that reminds us of our hurt, those painful old wounds reopen, and we suffer all over again.

In truth, the only salve that heals our pain is God's love. But we have to accept it. We have to open the doors of our hearts and invite Jesus in.

Does this seem strange to you?

If it does, I understand.

My childhood memories were not good ones, and they affected me until I reached the age of forty-four and the amazing revelation of how much God loves me filled me with so much joy that I felt my heart would burst! And because of this infilling of God's love, I was able to quit judging my family, forgive those who had hurt me, and let go of my anger. And then came hope.

Before this sunrise when God's light came upon me, I had never thought about what my parents experienced growing up…and I had never tried to understand what happened to them to form their personalities into the adults they became.

God graciously gave me the realization of why my father never held me or told me that he loved me, why my mother could never be pleased by anyone in the family, and why my brother ignored me.

> *You indeed are my savior,*
> *and in the shadow of your wings*
> *I shout for joy.*
> *Yet I am always with you;*
> *you take hold of my right hand.*

~ PSALMS 63:8, 73:23

Now I know why sitting outside my brother's room and gazing upon that statue of Jesus brought me such comfort. I now understand that Jesus was sitting there with me. He was holding my hand.

How do I know?

Time enlightened me.

ॐ ◆ ಛ

Reflection

"But to you who hear I say, love your enemies, do good to those who hate you, bless those who curse, pray for those who mistreat you" (Luke 6:27–28).

Chapter Five

THE SECOND STONE

When I was three years old, Dad moved our family from Tulsa to Lafayette, Louisiana. We lived there for about six months.

One day, Mother took me to play with a little girl about my age. My first playmate! Yeah!

While our mothers visited in another room, my new friend suggested we get under the dining room table and hide. The table had a tablecloth on it, which hung almost to the floor; and we were laughing and having so much fun as we crawled around under one end of the table and the other, pretending our moms couldn't see us. Suddenly my knee hit something sharp, and I cried out. Looking over at my playmate, I saw the look of fear on her face.

Of course, our mothers came running into the room, and my playmate's mother jerked up the tablecloth so they could see what was going on.

"Where did that glass come from?" my playmate's mother asked. Then looking at her daughter, she said, "That glass broke in the kitchen; how did it get in here? Why did you take it out of the garbage?"

Had my new friend really taken the broken glass out of the garbage and put it where I could get hurt? If so, why? Had the "slings and arrows" of life already hit her so hard that she was willing to hurt me? Or did she get blamed for something she didn't do?

I will never know. All I knew then was my "yeah" had turned into a "bam" and a "bah."

The scar from that day on my knee is a reminder of how we carry scars in our hearts from the "broken glass" that cuts us. Luckily for me, my scar is superficial, as are my feelings for that little playmate. Why? Because I carry no anger in my heart about what happened. But looking back on the incident, I know it influenced who I am today.

If she did indeed intend to hurt me, how many times have I done the same to hurt others?

How many times have I hurt someone because of something that happened in my past? Something not dealt with and/or forgiven?

Everything that has happened in our lives molds us into who we are today.

☙ ◆ ❧

Reflection

"As face mirrors face in water, so the heart reflects the person" (Proverbs 27:19).

Chapter Six

IN THE ARMS OF ANGELS

About a month after I got hurt on my first "play date," Dad moved our family back to Tulsa and into our old house, and it was there that God blessed me with an amazing gift. He gave me the knowledge that He really exists.

How did He do this?

Shortly before my fourth birthday, I fell quite ill with rubella. In those days, there was no vaccine to prevent German measles, and the symptoms could be very serious. In my case, the symptoms were so severe that even light would make me cry because my eyes hurt so much.

In those days, doctors made house calls; and our family physician, Dr. Bradley, came by to see me. Following his examination, he told my very concerned parents, "Most likely, she will not make it through the night." He then excused himself to make another house call, promising he would return as soon as he could.

When Mother came back into my bedroom, she was crying. She knelt down beside my bed and began to pray.

"Mommy," I called out her, "do you see them?"

"What do you see, Joan?" my mother asked.

"The angels, they've come for me."

"Oh, no!" she cried out.

Smiling, I reached up to take an angel's hand. In that instant, a feeling of peacefulness overcame me, and I realized I was floating with the angels above my room. Looking down, I could see my body still on the bed, and my mother beside it, still kneeling and crying as she prayed.

The angel holding my hand said to me, "You have to go back."

Now the overwhelming peacefulness began slipping away, and I begged, "*Please* don't make me."

"You have to—it's not time," the angel replied. And then they were gone.

I sat up in bed and either coughed up or vomited lots of green stuff.

When Dr. Bradley returned, he said, "Joan has made a miraculous recovery."

> *He took along the child's father and mother*
> *and those who were with him*
> *and entered the room where the child was.*
> *He took the child by the hand and said to her,*
> *"Talitha koum," which means,*
> *"Little girl, I say to you, arise!"*
> *The girl, a child of twelve, arose immediately*
> *and walked around.*
> *[At that] they were utterly astounded.*

~ MARK 5:40–42

Of course, there are people who have told me, "You dreamed it; you were only a child; you were very ill and probably delirious—it never happened."

But I know it wasn't a dream.

I am convinced these events are real because God grants miracles to give us hope; and on this night, He gave me a store of hope that I would need to call upon later in my life. And in His abundant generosity, He brought healing to my mother—a woman who bore so many deep wounds from the sticks and stones that had pummeled her in life. On this night, He graciously answered her sobbing prayers.

We know a miracle by its good fruits. In the arms of the angels, I realized a joy impossible to experience in our world so full of pain; and in those moments,

I understood God is *real*, and I wanted to go with the angels because they were returning to Him, who is Perfect Happiness.

That night as my mother knelt at my bedside, she experienced God's abiding love, and her relationship with Him was deepened.

These are the good fruits.

Seventy-five years later, I still have no doubt in my mind that God exists, just as I know that what I have shared with you here is true.

Reflection

"No evil shall befall you, no affliction come near your tent. For he commands his angels with regard to you, to guard you wherever you go" (Psalms 91:10–11).

Chapter Seven

THE THIRD STONE

Not long after my near-death experience, Dad moved the family to Jackson, Mississippi. For the second time in my life, I had someone to play with. My new little friend lived two houses down from us, and we had lots of fun playing together with dolls and my dollhouse...but as things turned out, we only got to play together a few times because of an incident involving the neighbors next door.

Since our neighborhood had no sidewalks, my friend and I would often cut through the next-door neighbors' yard to play with each other. One day while I was cutting through their property,

I accidentally stepped on something painfully sharp. Tacks! Three of them! Stuck into my bare foot!

You may wonder why I was barefoot and alone that afternoon. In those days, things were quite different than they are today. Children routinely ran barefoot and roamed freely (alone and with friends) about their neighborhoods; they rode bikes without helmets and played for hours away from home without causing their parents worry. Life was simpler then, more relaxed and more innocent.

The young couple who lived in the house next door didn't like us running through their yard; and so after I stepped on the tacks, my mother accused the lady of intentionally putting them in her yard. I remember seeing the look on her face when my mother spoke to her…it was the same look of fear in her eyes that I saw in the eyes of my first little playmate after I got cut by the broken glass under her dining room table. What happened that day inflicted another blow in my ability to trust, and it was one that would have a lasting effect on me.

Over the years, I have come to realize that sometimes things are not what they appear to be; and in reflecting on this incident and wondering what misery could have caused the next-door neighbors to be so mean to two five-year-olds, the thought occurred to me, *what if they hadn't put the tacks in their yard? What if someone else had put them there because they were mad at those people, or perhaps mad at my parents or me?*

I will never know the answer; but God is Mercy Himself, and thinking about this experience in a different light took away the pain and any anger still lingering in my heart.

> *We pray for mercy and in seeking it for ourselves,*
> *we learn to be mercy.*[3]
>
> ~ WILLIAM SHAKESPEARE

My family moved two months later.

If the person responsible for putting the tacks in the yard had exercised patience, they would not have had to live with the guilt of hurting me.

Regrets are hard to live with.

৪০ ◆ ৫৪

Even before I experienced the gift of God's peace in my life—my Sunrise—I always harbored feelings of sadness toward my first little playmate and the neighbors with the tacks in their yard. I grieve for those who go through life with such bitterness in their hearts.

> *To forgive is to set a prisoner free*
> *and discover that the prisoner was you.*
>
> ~ LEWIS B. SMEDES

There are two ways to hang from a gallows: either physically or emotionally. For more than half of my life, I hung emotionally in bitterness and unforgiveness that strangled my heart—bitterness and unforgiveness born from the pain of an ego bruised by the stones that were flung at me.

I confess that mostly my feelings were directed toward my mother. I adopted a "poor me" attitude. It was easier to be absorbed in my own self-pity than to try and understand why people acted the way they did.

ඥ ◆ ℭଃ

Reflection

"But when the kindness and generous love of God our savior appeared, not because of any righteous deeds we had done but because of his mercy, he saved us through the bath of rebirth and renewal by the Holy Spirit" (Titus 3:4–5).

· PART TWO ·

He who enters into the secret place
of his own soul passes himself,
and does in truth ascend to God.

~ SAINT ALBERT THE GREAT ~

Chapter Eight

A NEW DAWN

*We can only appreciate
the miracle of a sunrise
if we have waited in the darkness.*

~ UNKNOWN

Because of her own insecurities, Mother wanted me to be perfect. Of course, that wasn't humanly possible, and I resented her for trying to make me into someone I wasn't. As a result, feelings of unforgiveness and bitterness burdened my heart and affected me every day of my life...until that day when

I was 44 years old…the day God graciously answered my prayers and filled me with His Holy Spirit.

How did this transformation happen?

During a conversation with my dear friend Millie, she said to me, "You do not know Jesus."

Indignantly, I retorted, "Yes, I do! I have known Him all of my life! I go to church every Sunday."

"Yes," she replied, "but you do not *know* Him."

Little did I know then how right she was.

ଓ ◆ ଔ

Shortly after my conversation with Millie, my brother and I traveled to Tulsa to take care of Aunt Betty, who was struggling with Alzheimer's disease. On the way, my brother stopped at a Christian bookstore; and while I browsed through the books, one jumped out at me. It was a book written by a priest during a time when he felt burned out and depressed. As he sat on the floor praying for God's help, God touched his heart and filled it with the Holy Spirit, and the man was overcome by the feeling of complete peace. From then on, this priest walked with God on fire in His love.

When I returned home, I immediately went to Millie's house and told her about the book and my new understanding of God's love for each and every person who had ever lived. At the end of our visit as Millie walked with me to my car, these words came out of my mouth, but they were from deep within my heart, "Millie, I want to be filled with God's love; I want a personal relationship with Jesus."

She stopped and looked at me; and then she said, "Why not now?" And standing in her front yard, she began to pray.

In that moment, God's love filled me with a peace and contentment such as I had never felt before.

SUNRISE! THE LIGHT OF GOD.

The darkness that had controlled me was gone.

The realization was evident. My friend was right. Until that moment, I had not known God; I had not walked with Jesus as my friend. He had always seemed to be "out there" somewhere, not with me…not in me. And because of my own feelings of insecurity, I never understood or accepted how much He loves me.

God gave me an amazing gift that day: In that moment, like Saint Augustine, I could with my whole heart pray, "Late have I loved You….And see, You were in me, but I was outside…You were with me, but I was not with You….You touched me and I am set on fire for Your peace."[4]

৪০ ◆ ෬

Sometimes the gift of the Holy Spirit is given in a thunderclap, as mine was; sometimes the gift is given little by little, tenderly, because God, in His infinite love and wisdom, understands we are all different, and He knows what we need. However, no matter how the Holy Spirit is given to us, the results are the always the same: We realize unflinchingly that God is in our life, and we walk with Him who loves us. No matter what we may do to drive Him away, His love does not diminish. As I gradually came to accept this, I got to know and trust Him; and as I did, my love for Him deepened.

How do you fall in love with God?

Like all relationships, it takes time—time reading the Bible and other spiritual books; time praying; time spent quietly, listening to our inner voice, which is where God speaks to us. Learning to hear His voice means we have to be quiet so we can "hear" Him over the noise of life and our own thoughts.

Learning to hear Him means we have to ask God for His guidance. He always answers us—sometimes in that inner voice we hear only with our hearts, sometimes in a thought we know comes only from God, sometimes in messages conveyed through people or circumstances. But we cannot understand what God tells us unless we grow our relationship with Him. Love requires commitment. Commitment requires work. Work requires effort. Effort requires sacrifice. Love without work cannot flourish. Love without sacrifice dies.

As I gave God more of my time and attention, I began trusting Him, and I asked Him to help and guide me. I began to understand why He gave us Jesus, His Beloved Son, to walk with us on our journey, our journey to Him Who is Love. And as I trusted Him more, I loved Him more. He gave me hope.

Why?

Because He unconditionally validated me with His unconditional love.

> *In this way, the love of God was revealed to us:*
> *God sent his only Son into the world*
> *so that we might have life through him.*
> *In this is love: Not that we have loved God,*
> *but that he loved us and sent his Son*
> *as expiation for our sins.*
>
> ~ 1 JOHN 4:9–10

Love. Sacrifice. Trust. Hope. I wanted with all of my heart to have a relationship with God; and in His infinite love, He gave me the gift of a loving relationship with Him.

৪৹ ◆ ৪৺

It is difficult to feel validated as a worthy person by other people because most people are not whole themselves. We all have been hit by the sticks and stones of life; often, we don't know how or are too afraid to love (forget about unconditionally!).

It is easy to believe that no one is worthy of our trust; and it can be easy to believe God can't be trusted, either. But Jesus is always waiting at the door to our hearts...waiting to be invited in.

> *Behold, I stand at the door and knock.*
> *If anyone hears my voice and opens the door,*
> *[then] I will enter his house*
> *and dine with him, and he with me.*

~ REVELATION 3:20

Jesus waits even when we turn our backs on Him. He is at the door of our hearts, always knocking, because God is Pure Love, and Love does not walk away.

※ ◆ ↺

Reflection

"Commit your way to the LORD; trust in him and he will act And make your righteousness shine like the dawn, your justice like noonday" (Psalms 37:5–6).

Chapter Nine

FORGIVENESS

*If we really want to love,
we must learn to forgive.*

~ MOTHER TERESA OF CALCUTTA

When we forgive, we put on the face God gave us. I did not understand this when the Holy Spirit came to me on that beautiful day in Millie's front yard…but God soon led me to this truth.

ಙ ◆ ಚ

For me, the best way of getting to know God is through Scripture reading; and reading the Bible had become a daily habit when I came across this passage in the New Testament: "Stop judging, that you may not be judged. For as you judge, so will you be judged, and the measure with which you measure will be measured out to you" (Matthew 7:1–2).

Immediately, I said to myself, "I do not want to be judged by the same measure I am judging my mother."

God showed me that holding on to my past, not forgiving, was keeping me from growing deeper in my relationship with Him.

Forgiveness is a decision.

A few days later as I prayed The Lord's Prayer, I was struck by these words: *forgive us our trespasses as we forgive those who trespass against us*; and in that moment, God reminded me that I had to let go of my anger and forgive those who had hurt me.

Please God help me to forgive.

If we tell God that we truly want to forgive someone, He will graciously lead us to the place where we can forgive, and He will take away our pain so our hearts are freed.

When I finally made the decision to forgive, God gave me the gift to desire this with all my heart. But He wasn't done with me yet. Again while reading Scripture, He showed me this: "But I say to you, whoever is angry with his brother will be liable to judgment....Therefore, if you bring your gift to the altar, and there recall that your brother has anything against you, leave your gift there at the altar, go first and be reconciled with your brother, and then come and offer your gift" (Matthew 5:22–24).

Leave my gift at the altar?!

Lord, help me to be brave enough to reconcile with those who have hurt me.

By this time, God had freed me of most of the pain, hurt feelings, and anger that had festered within me for so many years; but in meditating and praying about this Biblical passage, I realized in my heart that Jesus was telling me to go to my mother and tell her I forgave her. In most circumstances, this would be a daunting task, but this was not hard for me to do because Mother was in a nursing home and suffering with late-stage Alzheimer's disease.

God is good, and He helped me. Holding Mother's hand in mine, I wept as I told her how much I loved her, and I asked her to forgive me for my failures. As I spoke softly to her, my forgiveness came from the depths of my heart; and although Mom didn't understand what I was saying, I did. For the first time in my life, I felt complete healing. Leaving the nursing home that day, the Sunrise that God had given me was even more vibrant and beautiful. My heart soared with absolute joy.

But still, God wasn't through with me.

A short time later, as I meditated on what Jesus said from the Cross, I was struck hard by these words:

> Then Jesus said, 'Father, forgive them,
> they know not what they do.'

~ LUKE 23:34

Of course! My mother did not realize what she had done, how she had hurt me. The stones of life had hit her hard. And then I understood. Because she felt unworthy, she had tried to make me perfect so everyone would like and accept me.

Carrying so much unforgiveness in my heart had kept me from realizing the beautiful gift Mother had given to me: my faith in God! She had taken my brother and me to church every Sunday, taught us to pray before meals and at bedtime, and what cherished gifts these were! In all the time I had spent feeling unnurtured, I had overlooked how she had nurtured my faith! And with that realization, the floodgates opened; and those tender moments with my mom, which I had blotted out of my memory for so long because of my anger, came flowing back to me.

That day, God gave me back my mother.

God is good.

ဢ ◆ ဢ

Before that beautiful day of my Sunrise when Millie prayed with me in her front yard, I never understood that God wants to be our best friend. He never leaves or gives up on us, no matter how much we reject Him, no matter how much we have sinned. He simply loves each one of us—and His love is unconditional.

God is here to help us. But we have to ask Him. He does not intrude or force Himself upon us. We have to invite Him in daily and talk to Him with a listening heart.

We all have someone we need to forgive…**and that goes for the failures we perceive in ourselves**. We need only to make the decision to forgive; God will take care of our pain.

ॐ ◆ ॐ

Reflection

"Father, forgive them, they know not what they do" (Luke 23:34).

Chapter Ten

A FLOOD OF MEMORIES

My father was a geologist for a small oil company, so we moved many times during my childhood...my guess is because in his job, he was always looking for oil. Moving was actually fun for me; I viewed it as an opportunity to see different places and meet new people. And although my early childhood was lonely, life changed when I was five years old and we moved to Evansville, Indiana.

Living in Evansville was a blessing because I finally had neighborhood friends to play with. The only thing is—they were all boys. There was not one girl in the neighborhood. So to keep up with the boys, I learned to climb trees, play shoot 'em up Wild West style, and kick the can.

Those days are now cherished memories of playing hide-and-go-seek and red rover, lying in the grass at night and looking up at the stars, riding bicycles, and searching for four-leaf clovers. I had so much fun during those four years in Evansville, not only with the neighborhood boys, but also with my classmate friends when I started school.

ꝏ ◆ ꞓ

We moved to Evansville a few weeks before December 7, 1941, the day the Japanese attacked Pearl Harbor. Although I had turned five just two months earlier, my memories of that day remain vivid. It was the day our lives changed. Within weeks, nearly every family in the country had a relative who had enlisted in the military services...and if not a family member, certainly, a good friend. And those of us who remained at home lived in constant fear that the doorbell would ring with news that our loved one was dead.

It was a time of fear; and in God, we place all of our hopes that neither Japan nor Germany would conquer us and that our loved ones would come home. And for those whose loved ones were dying, God was their consolation.

Almighty God: Our sons, pride of our Nation
this day have set upon a mighty endeavor,
a struggle to preserve our Republic, our religion,
and our civilization, and to set free a suffering
humanity. Lead them straight and true;
give strength to their arms, stoutness to
their hearts, steadfastness in their faith.
They will need Thy blessings.
Their road will be long and hard.
For the enemy is strong.
He may hurl back our forces.
Success may not come with rushing speed,
but we shall return again and again;
and we know that by Thy grace,
and by the righteousness of our cause,
our sons will triumph.[5]

~ FRANKLIN D. ROOSEVELT

When war came, there were still shortages in food, gasoline, and other materials. But no longer were they caused by the Depression. As Americans directed resources to supplying our troops and the war effort, families received ration books, which contained stamps that we used to buy the limited necessities still available to us, like food and gasoline. It was often a struggle, and I remember Mother having difficulty buying meat at the grocery store. To supplement the food we were able to purchase with ration stamps, she grew vegetables and canned them and went to a farm to buy cream so she could make butter.

This was the age before television; and every night, with bated breath, we huddled around the radio to listen to the news. Evansville was home to the nation's largest land-based naval shipyard as well as other manufacturing facilities, and we lived under constant threat of enemy attack. To protect us, civil defense officials conducted blackouts; and when these occurred, everyone had to turn out all of their lights.

ᙖ ◆ ᙗ

One of my most vivid memories of life in Evansville is the coal. It was the source of heat for every house and business in town; and in the winter, the smoke from burning coal was so thick in the air that if you left town and looked back, you could see a huge cloud of black soot hovering over the city.

During those long winter months in Indiana, we had to fill our furnaces with coal every day; and on very cold days, they had to be filled twice. At our house, the coal was stored in bins next to the furnace in our basement; and before refilling the furnace, my dad had to scrape the residue, or "clinkers" as we called them, out of the bottom of the furnace. It was a dirty business.

In those days, we did not have the convenience of modern-day appliances, and I recall Mom washing our clothes by hand and then putting them through a wringer to remove most of the water. The wringer washer was in our basement; and in the winter months, the basement was freezing cold, so Mom would bundle up to do the washing. It was too cold in Evansville in the wintertime to hang clothes outside to dry; they would simply freeze. And because of the sooty air, they would also get dirty, so Mother hung our wet clothes in the basement. It took them forever to dry, and so there were clothes hanging in our basement all winter long.

ဆ ◆ ભ

Shortly after we moved to Evansville, my first-grade teacher called Mother and told her I needed glasses. Sure enough, my eyesight was very poor. How poor? Well, when my parents took me to a movie after getting my glasses, I was so amazed, I blurted out in the theater, "Mommy, the people have faces just like we do!"

My glasses were very thick, and I endured lots of teasing because of them.

I was sick with earaches nearly every other week during the winter months, and it soon became obvious I was allergic to the coal smoke. This was before the discovery of penicillin; and the treatments for earaches were limited to eardrops, drinking sulfa, and laying on hot water bottles. The sulfa tasted terrible, and it was very hard to drink.

During my illnesses, I spent a lot of time in bed. Mother would call my teacher for the day's lessons and then teach me what they learned at school. She spent many hours lovingly teaching me how to multiply and divide fractions and how to read. And when my earaches hurt so badly they made me cry, she cared for my every need.

ℰℴ ◆ ℭℬ

On August 28, 1945, my brother celebrated his eighteenth birthday. At that time, all young men at the age of eighteen were required to register with the Selective Service and were then eligible for duty in the United States military. My brother was drafted.

It must have been terrible for my parents the day they put him on the train and watched him go off to boot camp…to a world unknown. I imagine they had to place their trust in God because there was nothing else they could do.

Fortunately, the war officially ended a few days later. September 2, 1945, was a day when our nation celebrated with horns honking and men and women weeping with joy. People streamed out of buildings and homes to hug each other and cheer and thank God for our hard-fought victory.

As things turned out, my brother did not come home for two years. He was sent to Japan where he served in the United States Army under General Douglas MacArthur and the allied occupational forces at the end of the war. But what a profound measure of gratitude Mother and Dad must have felt on that day because now they knew with certainty my brother would not be going into harm's way.

Such a flood of memories...all of which were blotted out of my mind until forgiveness unclouded my heart.

ℰ◆ℭ

Reflection

"Be strong and steadfast; have no fear or dread... for it is the LORD, your God, who marches with you; he will never fail you or forsake you" (Deuteronomy 31:6).

Chapter Eleven

THE LAST STONE

Shortly after the war ended, winter set in; and when furnaces started lighting up, my earaches began again. The doctors told my parents I might die if they didn't get me away from the coal smoke, so Dad asked for a transfer. We moved to Corpus Christi, Texas, right after Christmas.

Mom enrolled me in a private school that served grades elementary through junior high. I had attended the school for only a month when one day out on the playground, one of the middle-school students came up to me and began looking through my hair. "It *IS* dyed!" she announced. "It's a different color underneath!"

This was a traumatizing experience for me. First of all, because I didn't know this girl, and in those days, if you dyed your hair, you were considered immoral. But most of all, I was traumatized because my hair was not dyed...I was only ten years old.

One of my classmates had started the rumor. She had a habit of telling stories about other people—most of them untrue. In my case, people may have believed her because I was born with what everyone said was a beautiful shade of auburn. As the rumor about me spread through the school, the middle school girls had obviously been egged on by the sensationalism; however, the girl who ran her fingers through my hair seemed particularly intent on confirming the stories about me...perhaps she was jealous. Why else would she have behaved in such a way?

Why do people feel good when they hurt other people? Perhaps because they have been hit by stones that bruised their egos. Perhaps they think, *if I put you down, I'm better than you.*

ᏏᎤ ◆ ᏉᎦ

Shortly after the incident on the playground, my teachers became aware that I was having hearing difficulties, and they reported this to my mother.

Another trip to the doctor!

All of the ear infections I'd experienced in Indiana had left scar tissue on my eardrums, and my hearing was severely impaired. The doctor said I needed hearing aids.

Mother did not want me wearing hearing aids, so the doctor suggested another procedure that he said might help; however, he did not advise it because the long-term effects were unknown.

Mother asked the doctor to proceed with the cauterization procedure. She didn't like the idea of me having to wear hearing aids. My glasses were bad enough. As you recall, she wanted a smart, beautiful, perfectly dressed, eloquent daughter. But life was throwing enough stones in my direction that it was becoming obvious I would not measure up to her expectations. As time passed, I gradually lost all of my self-confidence.

The doctor performed the procedure as my mother requested. It involved running a stick of radiation up both of my nostrils to burn away the scar tissue, which it did. As I was undergoing this procedure, I remember wondering, *what if this affects my brain?* A short time later, the procedure was banned.

৪০ ◆ ৪১

We are products of everything that happens to us. Unfortunately, life's bruises often impact us more than the love we receive. If we keep reinjuring our bruises with unforgiveness, they never heal.

When I forgave my mother, I had to also forgive the little playmate who put the broken glass under her table, the couple with the tacks in their yard, the girl who started the rumor that my hair was dyed, and everyone else who had ever hurt me. To fail to forgive even one of them would simply prolong my pain. I would not heal.

There are sixty-four Scriptural passages in the Bible that tell us we are "wonderfully made." When I made the decision to forgive, a huge weight was lifted from my bruised heart, and I was healed. The freedom I experienced afterwards helped me to finally accept that I was wonderfully made. God has "wonderfully made" all of us. That means you and me and everyone who has ever lived.

80 ◆ 03

Reflection

"You formed my innermost being; you knit me in my mother's womb. I praise you, because I am wonderfully made; wonderful are your works! My very self you know. My bones are not hidden from you, When I was being made in secret, fashioned in the depths of the earth. Your eyes saw me unformed; in your book all are written down; my days were shaped, before one came to be" (Psalms 139:13–16).

Chapter Twelve

OUT OF DIFFICULTIES

Because the gossip continued about my hair being dyed, Mother enrolled me in public school at the start of seventh grade. I could tell that Mom really understood how hard it was for me to face those girls who were hurting me at school; and I thought to myself, *she does love me*!

Ironically, when I reached the eighth grade, the girl who started the rumors about me switched to the public school I was attending, and she was the bane of my existence all the way through high school. However, by the time I reached high school, I was surrounded by many friends and had lots of dates.

Unfortunately, things were not any easier at home. Mom's insecurities were getting worse with age; and during my high school years, she transferred her insecurities to me by criticizing everything I said and did, even what I wore, and I began to feel very self-conscious in public. I realized even then that Mother did not intend to hurt me when she said things like, "You aren't going to wear that to school," and "Why did you say what you said; that was not the correct way to talk," and "Go comb your hair. It looks terrible."

How did I know she didn't mean to hurt me? Because when I came home from school, there would be new clothes lying on my bed. That was Mom's way of telling me she loved me. Still, her words stung; and I would find myself thinking, *this does not take away the hurt for what you said this morning.* I understood that buying things does not make one happy or heal the deep interior pain that festers in one's heart.

By the time I was fourteen, I realized Mother treated Dad the same way she treated me. They fought almost every night because he couldn't please her, either. There were tears many nights, and it was either Dad or I who was the cause of her unhappiness. At some point during this tumultuous time, I realized Dad and I were taking the brunt of her childhood pain; and I remember one night promising God (and it is my prayer I have kept that promise), "I will *never* do to my children what my mother is doing to me."

On the way home from school one afternoon, I felt a tug on my heart and the urge to stop at the church; and although I didn't know why at the time, I pulled over, parked, and went in. I just sat in a pew and looked at Jesus on the Cross. I have no idea how long I sat there or what thoughts went through my mind, but I know looking at His suffering somehow made my suffering bearable.

Perhaps Jesus wanted me to understand "Whoever does not carry his own cross and come after me, cannot be my disciple,"[6] or maybe God wanted me to understand that He was "walking with me and holding me by the right hand."[7] Or perhaps God wanted me to understand both Scripture verses because He knew I would one day bear the cross of illness, and He wanted me to know He would be there with me.

଼ ◆ ଽ

Reflection

"Be strong and take heart, all who hope in the LORD" (Psalms 31:25).

Chapter Thirteen

J ERRY

Out of difficulties, grow miracles.

JEAN DE LA BRUYERE

My college days were spent at the University of Texas. Mom wanted me to join a sorority; but because I lacked self-confidence, I dreaded the prospect. Going through rush was very stressful, but I managed to get accepted to the sorority Mother had selected for me.

Sorority life did nothing to improve my feelings of inferiority; but I did gain one precious gift from the experience: my "little sorority sister," Mary Ann, who became my cherished friend. Our lifelong friendship reminds me, "Beneath every cloud, there is a silver lining."

Following college graduation, Mary Ann and I found work in Houston, and we rented an apartment together. It was during this time that I met the man who would become the love of my life.

ଽୠ◆ଓଷ

When I met Jerry, he had recently been discharged from active duty in the United States Navy. His sister lived in Houston, so he moved there to look for work. His brother-in-law and nephew drove him around for several days looking at apartments; and when he came to the apartment complex where I lived, he ran into another young man who was looking for a roommate to share expenses.

Jerry knew this was the place he needed to be; and after a long, hot day of moving, he went down to the pool at the complex to swim and relax. As it happened, I had a date that evening; and following the movie, my date Arthur and I went out to the pool to enjoy the night air. Jerry was the only other person there, and he and Arthur struck up a conversation.

We had not been poolside very long when Jerry said to Arthur, "Let's see who can swim underneath the water the longest."

Well, Arthur, with his huge ego, naturally said, "Sure!" and jumped in.

While Arthur was swimming (showing off), Jerry and I talked. When it was Jerry's turn, he swam only one lap; then he climbed out of the pool and challenged Arthur to swim again. Of course, Arthur did, and Jerry and I talked some more. Sometime during our conversation, the thought entered my head, *this man is going to be important in my life*.

Have you ever experienced something like this? Where do you think the thought came from?

I have no doubt but that God whispered that thought in my ear; and after that night, Arthur was no longer a part of my life.

From then on, every night after work, Jerry and I would sit by the pool and talk, and then he would cook dinner for me. We didn't go out on formal dates, but we didn't need to. Jerry had just started a new job and didn't have a lot of money; and this turned out to be a wonderful thing because instead of going places, we got to know each other by sharing our life stories, our thoughts, hopes, and dreams. Very quickly, our friendship grew into a deep and abiding bond.

Three weeks after we met, the company I worked for informed me that I was being transferred to New Orleans. That evening when I told Jerry my news, the conversation went like this:

Jerry: "You can't go."

Me: "The only way to tell them I can't go is to tell them I'm getting married."

Jerry: "You don't want to marry me; I'm poor."

Me: "I don't care about money."

Jerry: "Will you marry me?"

Me: "Yes!"

It was the happiest night of my life.

෯ ◆ ෬

On reflection, I now realize that God used my less-than-perfect childhood to teach me a valuable lesson: to put aside things that hinder a relationship. Although I didn't understand it at the time, everything in my life had taught me neither money nor social position is the source of true joy.

> *For where your treasure is,*
> *there also will your heart be.*
>
> ~ LUKE 12:34

Was it a coincidence that Jerry ended up in the apartment complex where I lived? Or that no one but Jerry was at the pool that night when Arthur and I returned from our date?

Albert Einstein has been quoted as saying, "Coincidence is God's way of remaining anonymous," and Friedrich Schiller wrote, "There is no such thing as chance; and what seems to us mere accident springs from the deepest source of destiny." Well there is no doubt in my mind or my heart that Jerry is my destiny, and how truly blessed I am to have shared my life with him for fifty-five golden years.

Of course, our journey has not been without its bumpy spots, and we have had our fair share of misunderstandings; but whenever two egos are involved, one cannot avoid disagreements. However, Jerry's wisdom has always kept things from escalating. He insists that we never rehash anything; it simply does no good. So if we argue about something, after speaking our minds, we smile at each other and move on with no hard feelings or grudges. We don't burden our relationship with unforgiveness or allow it to fester in our hearts.

೫ ◆ ೪

When my parents met Jerry, they both liked him; and my mother made me very happy when she told me, "He's so sweet."

We decided on a small wedding with just immediate family and a few close friends. Since my parents had moved from Corpus to Wichita Falls and knew very few people where they now lived, we decided to get married in Houston; and actually, that was a relief to me because there would be no worry about Mom getting uptight about impressing anyone.

Mary Ann was my maid of honor. Jerry's best friend from childhood was still in the service and could not attend, so my "little sister's" fiancé was Jerry's best man. When we exchanged our vows, Jerry and I looked into each other's eyes and accordingly, into each other's hearts; and we promised God to honor, to love, and to hold each other "until death do us part." As we walked down the aisle toward the back of the church and into our life together, I felt as though my heart would burst with love for this man who was now my husband.

God is my treasure and my joy, and He blessed me with the gift of Jerry, who still has my heart.

ßひ ◆ ௸

Reflection

"He will love and bless and multiply you; he will bless the fruit of your womb and the produce of your soil, your grain and wine and oil, the young of your herds and the offspring of your flocks, in the land which he swore to your ancestors he would give you" (Deuteronomy 7:13).

Chapter Fourteen

CHILDREN

A year after Jerry and I were married, our daughter Kathy was born. Before she was delivered, we both nearly died. The doctor did not want to come to the hospital in the middle of the night, so the nurse gave me something to slow down my labor. The medication almost killed us.

A year and a half after Kathy was born, Linda arrived; and two years later, our son Scott was born. Fortunately, I had no trouble with their deliveries.

Those were happy and busy years. You can imagine what it was like taking care of three small children so close in age. We changed and washed diapers for four solid years, and we did it without a clothes dryer until after Scott was born.

ಶಿ ♦ ෪

When Kathy was only ten months old, I realized in a very painful way that as parents we can traumatize our children.

Jerry was still in the Naval Reserves, and he had to attend a weeklong function. Naturally, he wanted me to go with him, and I wanted to go. So we took Kathy to my mother's for the week thinking she would be fine since my mother adored her. What we never expected was how Kathy would be traumatized by my absence.

When we got home from our trip, Jerry had to work so he put me on a train (since we had only one car), and I went to my mother's home to get Kathy.

I was so anxious to hold my baby that I could hardly wait; but when Kathy saw me, she began screaming and clung to my mother. She wouldn't look at me or come to me. I was heartbroken. It had never occurred to me that she would think we had deserted her. It wasn't until the next day that she let me hold her again...and when she did, I clung to her as she clutched me. I had never intended to hurt my baby. Nevertheless, she had been traumatized.

How many other times were my children affected by what I did?

How many times did I unintentionally hurt them?

How often are all children affected emotionally by parents who hurt them unintentionally or intentionally?

When going through my forgiveness list, I had to search for forgiveness of myself...forgiveness for all the mistakes I'd made, especially when my ego or desires triumphed over reason.

಄ ◆ ಖ

Reflection

"I prayed for this child, and the LORD granted my request. Now I, in turn, give him to the LORD; as long as he lives, he shall be dedicated to the LORD" (1 Samuel 1:27–28).

Chapter Fifteen

A FRAID OF THE DARK

One day while grocery shopping with my children, who were now four, three, and one, I suddenly felt faint. My first thought was, *what will happen to my children*? The fear that some harm could befall them should I be unable to care for them triggered a case of agoraphobia that lasted for four years.

Agoraphobia is an anxiety disorder that is characterized by feelings of intense fear in response to or in anticipation of situations such as using public transportation, being in open or enclosed spaces, standing in crowds, or being alone away from home. In my case, for a whole year, I was afraid to leave the house unless Jerry was with me; and even then, it was painfully difficult. Although I would not admit it to myself at the time, I have often thought that my agoraphobia may have been triggered by the feeling I was going to faint; but the deep underlying cause was this: I had no self-confidence in public due to the pressure my mother had put on me growing up.

The thought of going to church terrified me. I felt trapped like a scared rabbit. Why? Because there was no way to leave during Mass! So Jerry came up with the idea of sitting in the last row of the cry room; then if I was overcome by a panic attack, we could get up and leave and no one would notice. After sitting in the cry room for nearly a year, we were finally able to move to the last row of pews in the church.

It was the same everywhere we went. Finally, Jerry talked me into going to a movie, where we sat in the last row, and then to a restaurant, where I managed to sit through the meal with his constant and loving encouragement. It was sheer determination that enabled me to make it for Jerry's sake. He must have grown tired of dealing with this terrible illness; nevertheless, he was always wonderful in caring for me in his own patient way. Eventually, I got well, but I think it would have been impossible for me to overcome my agoraphobia had it not been for my dear husband's help. He was my rock.

Love is stronger than fear. There are 365 instances in the Bible that tell us, "Fear not!" When we give our fears to God, we overcome them. Love always wins.

And the closer we are to God, the less fear we have in our daily lives.

The children, although very young, remember this time in our lives. I do not know how it affected them, but it must have because they don't talk much about it. What Jerry and I know is that we have three beautiful, wonderful grown children who have made us very happy and proud.

ℰ◆ℛ

During those years that I was struggling with agoraphobia, Jerry and I loved to take the children to Galveston where we could walk the beaches and sit in the sand and watch the waves roll in. Those were truly wonderful times of listening to and watching the seagulls, searching for seashells, and relaxing as we watched our children play.

I never experienced any symptoms of agoraphobia while we were at the beach. There is something so calming about being near the water. And as Jerry sat beside me in those serene and glorious moments, my heart would recall what Jesus said to the woman at the well....

Everyone who drinks this water will be thirsty again;
but whoever drinks the water I shall give will never
thirst; the water I shall give will become in him a
spring of water welling up to eternal life.

~ JOHN 4:13–14

Jesus, You are the Living Water, the wellspring of Mercy and Compassion, wash over us, overwhelm us in Your love.

ଚ ◆ ଌ

Reflection

"Fear not...Do not worry about tomorrow; tomorrow will take care of itself" (Matthew 6:34).

Chapter Sixteen

A GLIMMER OF LIGHT

Jerry worked on straight commission; and one time when the economy was in a deep recession, our income fell significantly. I decided I needed to help him support our family by getting a job. The children were only ten, eight, and six; and forty-some years ago, there were no daycare places to leave them, so I wanted to find something that was part time. That way, my working hours could accommodate the needs of our family. And again, God was there for me. He gave me the perfect job.

The thought of ringing doorbells and selling Avon had never entered my mind, but a friend recommended me so she could qualify for a drawing, and her manager called me to see if I was interested in becoming an Avon sales representative. Much to my friend's surprise and Jerry's amazement, I said yes!

Knowing I still grappled with residual anxiety from the agoraphobia, Jerry said to me, "You won't be able to knock on doors."

"Watch me!" I answered.

The next day, after taking a deep breath, I knocked on my first door.

"Come in!" was the welcome that met me, and then I got my first big order!

After that, nothing held me back.

Where did my courage and determination come from? God, of course! Why? Because I was helping my husband; and although he never asked me to help support our family, for me, getting a part-time job was an act of love. And God, being pure Love, held my hand as I walked out of my house and knocked on the first front door.

ಹಿ ◆ ೞ

I sold Avon for nineteen years. What a blessing it was. Many wonderful things came from being a sales rep: I met lifelong friends by knocking on their doors; I learned to be a good listener when they confided their problems to me; and because I could arrange my working hours around the needs of my children, I didn't need to leave them with a babysitter. I was home when they were.

And one of the biggest blessings? I overcame my agoraphobia.

Looking back, I can see that God was always present. He is always present in your life, too. Although we may not recognize Him, He waits for us to ask Him to be a part of our lives. He loves us and wants to help us. But He will not intrude. He will not overtake our lives. He gave us free will. I could have said no to the offer of selling Avon, and my life would have been completely different. Perhaps the fear of that day in the grocery store would have returned.

When I was offered the sales job with Avon, it was easy to accept because, in my heart, I knew it was the right thing to do. When we pray and invite Jesus into our hearts, we can listen with our hearts and follow our hearts' desires with confidence and peace of mind.

One of the biggest blessings I received by selling Avon was my friendship with Millie, who said, "You do not know God." Millie's life was not an easy one to live, but she was always joyful; no matter what was happening, she exuded peacefulness. After my own experience of getting to know God and inviting Him to be a part of my life, I began to understand how Millie could exhibit such peace when things were going so terribly wrong. It was because she walked and talked with God. And her faith and trust in Him were the gifts she imparted to me with the simple statement, "You do not know Him."

ॐ ◆ ☙

Reflection

"Make known to me your ways, LORD; teach me your paths. Guide me by your fidelity and teach me, for you are God my savior, for you I wait all the day long" (Psalms 25:4–5).

Chapter Seventeen

Brilliance

After my Sunrise, I began to clear the garbage out of my inner self. Of course, there were things to be dealt with that made my heart heavy.

One day, I came across an article written by a doctor that read, "A smile makes you happy inside and keeps you young."

My thought was, *I wonder if it works*.

So off to the mall I went, and there I began walking from one end to the other—the whole distance—with a big smile on my face. I smiled at everyone I met. And lo, guess what! Everyone smiled back.

That day, God reminded me of something I already knew but hadn't actually thought much about. Every one of the people I saw received a gift— a smile; but my gift was greater—I received twenty smiles, and the feeling I had after initiating so many smiles cheered me up and made my heart feel good.

It is more blessed to give than to receive.

ACTS 20:35

That day's smile exercise has gradually overtaken my life, and here is what I have learned: A smile can make an unhappy person happy; a smile is sometimes better than words.

Have you ever comforted someone who was weeping by simply smiling at them? What did you get in return?

A smile!

The deeds you do may be the only
sermon that people hear today....
Preach the Gospel always;
if necessary, use words.

~ SAINT FRANCIS OF ASSISI

Walking down the mall and smiling at people was the last thing I wanted to do; but when that day had ended, there was a smile on my face and in my heart. God blessed me that day with a blessing that lasted.

ℰ ◆ ℬ

Reflection

"Then all who trust in you will be glad and forever shout for joy. You will protect them and those will rejoice in you who love your name" (Psalms 5:12).

· PART THREE ·

Let us love the Cross,
and let us remember that we are not alone
in carrying it.
God is helping us.

~ Saint Gianna Beretta Molla ~

ଯ ♦ ଓ

Chapter Eighteen

THE UNEXPECTED

We had been living in the Texas Hill Country only one year when I was diagnosed with stage IV melanoma. Before my diagnosis, several doctors had told me the spot on my scalp was nothing to worry about; but in my heart, I knew something was wrong. Finally, after I requested it, the last doctor I saw performed a biopsy on the growth.

A few days later, while I was sitting at my desk, the phone rang. It was the doctor, who told me over the phone I had stage IV melanoma. Cancer is something I had never worried or even thought about until the growth popped up on the top of my head. No one in my family had cancer.

The things I had worried about never happened. Cancer was a complete surprise.

I put down the phone and slowly got up and walked into the den. Jerry was sitting on the couch, working on his laptop. I sat down next to him and said, "Honey, I have something I have to tell you."

He looked up at me; concern etched his face.

"I have stage IV melanoma."

His response was shock. "What do we do?"

"I guess, call the doctor he told me to call," I responded, a little surprised there was no fear in my heart. I was blessed to be able to say to God as I rose from the couch, "I am not ready to die; but if You are ready to take me, it's okay."

ଞ ◆ ଔ

We went to see the doctor and set a date to remove the melanoma. A week after the surgery, the doctor called to tell me he had not gotten clean margins, and so I underwent another procedure. A week following the second surgery, the doctor called again to tell me he still hadn't gotten clean margins; and so a week after that, I underwent yet another procedure.

The third time was a charm, but then the doctor recommended I undergo radiation treatments, and Jerry and I decided to follow his advice. Before my first treatment, the doctor told me to have my head shaved.

Because of the three operations, I had skin grafts on the top of my head, so I knew there would never be hair there again. Nevertheless, on the day I visited my beautician, as she began shaving my head, tears ran down my cheeks.

Well, those of you who have had radiation know what comes next. When I went for the first visit, they laid me down on a table. And the next thing I knew, they had strapped me down and put a mask over my face. "We have to take a mold of your head so we can fit a device to hold your head in place when we do the radiation," the technician told me.

છ ◆ ૪૭

Before my first radiation treatment, they placed the device over my head and screwed it down to the table. *Oh great*, I thought. *Can I do this?* Talk about trying to control a panic attack! How did I manage to do this five days a week for four weeks?

Prayer.

I asked Jesus to help me when the terror of my head being secured to the table overtook me, and then I thought about how He must have felt when He was tied to a pillar and beaten. Connecting my cross to His Cross calmed my nerves enough to let the radiologist put the mask over my face and fasten it to the table.

After the first two weeks, it was easier to joke about my situation by saying things like, "If the building catches on fire, don't forget to unscrew my head before you leave," or thinking to myself, *I'm the lady in the iron mask.*[8]

During the last two days of my radiation treatments, two more growths appeared on my head. Following my final treatment, the doctor called Jerry and me in to his office. He examined the two new growths and said, "Go home and enjoy." Then as his voice trailed off, he looked down and left the examining room.

A death sentence?

Jerry and I looked at each other; then he took my hand and helped me off of the table, and we walked out the door. There was no crying, nor was there any anger or bitterness in our hearts.

Thank You Sweet Jesus for giving us a peaceful walk to the car and a serene ride home.

൩ ◆ ೞ

Reflection

"Though my flesh and my heart fail, God is the rock of my heart, my portion forever" (Psalms 73:26).

Chapter Nineteen

A YEAR OF BLESSINGS

When my original doctor was informed about my medical status, he called me. He said he had made an appointment for me at MD Anderson in Houston for the following Monday. Throughout my illness, Jerry had wanted me to go to MDA for treatment; but I had resisted, instead wanting to stay home in Austin. However, when the doctor told me MDA was my only chance, I finally agreed.

God gave me a wonderful doctor at MDA. He came in, checked me over, and told Jerry and me about a new experimental treatment. In order to kill all of the melanoma, it would take me close to death every time they administered it. During our visit, the doctor also implied my cancer was advanced, and so it might be too late for the treatment to help me.

The oncologist spent three hours with us evaluating my condition. Then he left to talk over my case with some of his colleagues. After awhile, four other doctors came in and examined me. When they left, the original doctor returned. "They think you should do the treatment," he said.

Again, he emphasized the treatment could kill me; but really, there was no alternative decision to make. I would definitely die without doing something to kill the melanoma in my body. At least by doing the treatment, there was hope.

ಬಿ ◆ ೞ

What followed was a year of terrible chemo.

I was admitted to the hospital for a week each time. They would administer five kinds of chemo and two kinds of biotherapy for seven days. Then they would send me home for three weeks to recuperate, and Jerry would give me white blood cell shots to try to restore my immune system for the next treatment. After three weeks, I would return to MDA for the next round.

During these treatments, I had no control and gradually lost all my dignity. And yet because of the lesson I had learned that day in the mall, I was able to smile through all of it. My nurses even commented to Jerry, "We have never seen anyone smile like she does with all that she is going through." And of course, prayers helped. In my darkest moments, I could actually feel my wonderful friends' prayers for me, and their love joined with God's love would overwhelm me with complete peace.

No matter how dark it seems, if you can trust God, you will witness His many blessings. The chemo treatments were not only difficult, they caused hallucinations. When I felt one coming on, I would pray, "Dear Lord, please don't allow this to be a bad one," and in His love, He graciously answered my prayers. Instead of being frightening, my hallucinations were beautiful. I would envision myself walking down a path and observe something golden on the ground; and upon approaching it, the object would rise up, and it would be an angel with golden hair. Or I would see the Holy Family—Jesus, Mary, and Joseph—up in the sky with beautiful stars shining all around them. And sometimes, in my half-conscious state, I would hear a soft voice whispering in my ear, "Do you trust me?" and I would say, "Yes, Lord, I trust You."

> *Always remember, the future comes*
> *one day at a time.*
>
> ~ DEAN ACHESON

Trust gave me the courage to look to the future. And for me during my treatments, the future came one minute at a time.

৪০ ◆ ೮৪

One day while I was waiting for a CT scan, a young woman said to me, "In Japan, they fight melanoma with shiitake mushrooms."

In my weak voice I replied, "They do?"

She then asked for Jerry's phone number and called him for his email address. After that, she sent him the address for the website where he could purchase shiitake mushroom pills online. Subsequently, she repeatedly pestered him until he finally ordered the pills. Afterwards, he never heard from her again.

Because of complications, I had to stop chemo treatments early, and I returned to the oncologist for a decision on the two melanomas that had popped up on my head. When he examined me, the doctor exclaimed, "They've shrunk! That doesn't happen after we quit chemo."

৪০ ◆ ೮৪

Was it a coincidence that the melanomas shrank? Was the young woman who gave me the advice about shiitake mushrooms an angel from God?

We can choose to believe whatever we are comfortable with. As for me, my heart tells me that God was a part of all of this. Jesus walked with me and held my hand.

ಐ ◆ ೞ

God gave me many blessings during my treatments, but the biggest and most wonderful blessing occurred during my fourth treatment. It was a revelation—not just for me but also for you, and it is a blessing He wants to give to each and every one of His children....

ಐ ◆ ೞ

Reflection

"They that hope in the LORD will renew their strength, they will soar on eagles' wings; They will run and not grow weary, walk and not grow faint" (Isaiah 40:31).

Chapter Twenty

Holding hands

During the week of my fourth treatment, I could no longer feel God's presence. I know God is not a feeling, and I knew He was still with me, but I was so ill, I needed to feel His presence. Knowing that MDA had a chapel, I asked Jerry to take me to Mass.

He reluctantly asked me, "Do you think you can sit in a wheelchair that long?"

When I assured him that I could, he put me into a wheelchair, but he had to tie me in because I was too weak to sit up. He was afraid I would fall forward and out onto the floor.

I didn't feeling anything different during the service; but when Mass was over, a woman—a complete stranger—walked up to me, took my hand, looked deeply into my eyes, and said, "Jesus gave me a message for you."

"He did?!" I was astounded.

"Yes. He said to tell you that He is holding your hand every step of the way."

When I thanked the woman for bringing me His message, she said to me, "I could never deny my Jesus anything He asks of me." Then she smiled and walked away.

I never saw her again.

How did she know out of all of the cancer patients at Mass that day to come to me? Only God knows. One thing is certain: God used her love for Him to bring me joy.

> *Tears of joy are like the summer rain drops*
> *pierced by sunbeams.*

> ~ HOSEA BALLOU

৪০ ◆ ৫৪

Reflection

"Rejoice in the Lord always. I shall say it again: rejoice! Your kindness should be known to all. The Lord is near. Have no anxiety at all, but in everything, by prayer and petition, with thanksgiving,

make your requests known to God. Then the peace of
God that surpasses all understanding will guard your
hearts and minds in Christ Jesus" (Philippians 4:4–7).

Chapter Twenty-One

IN HIS LOVE

The message God shared with me through the woman after Mass overwhelmed me and kept the light of His presence in my life as I walked the next fifteen years.

God will do for you what He did for me.

You may think, *Jesus will not do that for me*.

But Jesus said, "Ask and you shall receive."

Ask.

Ask for *what*? Receive *what*?

ঙ ◆ ଓ

Several years ago while I was waiting to have a mammogram, a middle-aged woman came into the changing room area. She had trouble opening the locker; so naturally, with all my years of experience in opening lockers, I offered to help her.

After she had changed into an examining gown, she sat down next to me.

"Have you had cancer before?" she asked me.

"Yes," I said. "Ten years ago, I had stage IV melanoma."

She immediately began sobbing, and I gently grasped her hand. Then she looked at me and said, "I asked God to put someone in my life who had survived stage IV cancer."

I didn't know how to respond, so I just kept holding her hand and looking at her with love. My heart was breaking for her.

"I have not been close to God," she confided.

She had not relied on God or walked with Him, and still, He had graciously given her what she asked when she desperately turned to Him.

God always answers us. Sometimes it is with a 'No', sometimes it is with a 'Yes', sometimes it is with a 'Wait, I have something so much better in mind for you'.

Ask and you shall receive. Even if you haven't turned to Him in the past, trust Him now. Pray for the gift to trust Him if you must. Pray it with the heart of a child. If you are deep in need and ask from the bottom of your heart, God will do for you what He did for me, what He did for that woman in the breast cancer diagnostic center.

Why? Because He loves you with all His heart.

ఠ◆ొ

Reflection

"'What do you want me to do for you?' The blind man replied, 'Master, I want to see'" (Mark 10:51).

Chapter Twenty-Two

Mᴏʀᴇ ᴄᴀɴᴄᴇʀ

You may ask why I was at MDA several years after completing my melanoma treatments. The answer is simple. I had developed lung cancer. And because my body could not handle any more chemo or radiation, the surgeon removed half of my lung. Following the surgery, Jerry took me home.

And the sun was shining.

When we returned to MDA for my postsurgical follow-up, the CT scan showed my lungs were full of something. I had no choice but to undergo a biopsy. We returned home and waited a week for the results...and we prayed. Many people in my parish blessed me with their prayers, too.

And the sun was shining.

When we returned to Houston to hear the biopsy results, the whole family went. I think Jerry and the children were afraid of the worst; so when we heard from the doctor, "It's a fungus," we all began hugging each other and thanking God for again graciously answering our prayers.

And the sun was shining.

However, three years later when I returned to MDA, the follow-up news was not so good. The CT scan showed I had breast cancer. But that wasn't all of it. We had always known there was a small opening on the top of my head from the melanoma surgeries. None of the operations or skin grafts had been able to close it. We were informed the CT scan also showed that air going through the small hole in my head for the past ten years had caused that area of my skull to disintegrate. If the doctors didn't correct this situation, the meninges protecting my brain would be exposed.

The doctors told us there was a new procedure that might work; however, it was experimental. It involved the surgeon taking a long muscle out of my back and tying it to the blood supply over my temple, then covering the muscle with skin grafts. In order for it to be successful, the blood supply had to flow all over the top of my head from where it was connected to my temple. The surgeons performed this procedure in tandem with the breast cancer surgery; it was a twelve-hour operation.

A few days following surgery, when a nurse drained the four large bags hanging on my chest, she forgot to pin them back to my gown. As I got out of bed, I felt a tug at my waist. I looked down to see what was happening just as the line popped, throwing me backwards about five feet. I hit my head on the wall and cut it open. In the fall, I also broke my hip.

Repairing my injuries required another long surgery and more stitches in my head, although luckily, in a different spot from my operation two days earlier. The hip surgery did not go well. The doctor had complications and did not repair the hip properly. To this day, my hip still hurts and one leg is shorter than the other; and as a result, I've developed curvature to my spine.

Are you wondering did we sue?

No.

Anyone can make a mistake, and my heart went out to that nurse who forgot to repin the drainage bags. As for the surgeon, once my femur started crumbling, he simply had to complete the surgery using wires the best he could.

I offered Jesus my pain, and He held my hand. And through all of this, *the sun was shining.*

I was in the hospital for a month. When they released me, I was still so weak they could barely get me in the car. Jerry and I drove away from the hospital on our fiftieth wedding anniversary. What a gift!

> *When the sun is shining,*
> *I can do anything;*
> *No mountain is too high,*
> *No trouble too difficult to overcome.*
>
> ~ WILMA RUDOLPH

And more gifts awaited me at home, like the wonderful caretakers I had, and the fact that I was able to get out of the wheelchair and walk five months later…and that, to this day, I remain cancer free.

God is good.

৪০ ◆ ෬

Reflection

"Therefore, we are not discouraged; rather, although our outer self is wasting away, our inner self is being renewed day by day" (2 Corinthians 4:16).

Chapter Twenty-Three

EVERY PERFECT GIFT

Three years after I had recovered from my breast cancer, graft, and hip replacement surgeries, I was getting ready one morning to attend a funeral. Suddenly, my left hand began shaking uncontrollably.

Parkinson's? I wondered.

Parkinson's disease affects the nerves in your brain, which in turn control every muscle in your body. With Parkinson's, your hands shake; it's difficult to make your feet move, especially when going through doorways; it affects your facial muscles making it harder to chew; and you may drool. Many people do not know that Parkinson's is caused by a lack of dopamine in the brain. Dopamine is what our brains use to send signals to the other parts of our bodies. It regulates all of our body movements as well as our emotions.

People ask me how I stay so positive and happy with all of the challenges I've faced in my life. Granted, not many people have faced stage IV melanoma, two types of lung cancer, breast cancer, seven major surgeries including hip replacement surgery, and then Parkinson's disease, but then some have faced so much more.

Here are my secrets. This is what I have learned.

Forgiveness is a decision. Forgive those who have hurt you, either intentionally or unintentionally. And forgive yourself.

The only salve that will heal your pain is God's love. If you tell God that you truly want to forgive someone, He will graciously lead you to the place where you can forgive, and He will take away your unhappiness so your heart is freed.

Recognize that God is always working in your life. For me, one of the most dramatic times I recognized His hand in my life was, of course, when I met Jerry. But there have been many times when I recognized His presence: when I took the job selling Avon, when the woman came up to me after Mass at MDA, when I held the hand of that woman as she wept over her illness—these are but a few times I have felt God's presence. But so many times, He has been there for me when I didn't realize it: when He sent His angels to me while I was so sick with rubella, when He called me to Him and I stopped at the church on my way home from school, when He invited me to make Him a bigger part of my life with Millie's challenge, "You don't know God."

Looking back, I see how He has "carried me" through my illnesses and the many challenges that I've faced throughout my life. And always, in good times and in bad, when I recognized Him and when I didn't, when I invited Him in and when I didn't, He has walked with me and loved me.

Pray for mercy, and in seeking it, you will learn mercy. Remember what Jesus said from the Cross. After hours of being beaten, spit upon, and having carried His heavy Cross to the place where they crucified Him, He prayed for those who had hurt Him. He prayed for us, whose sins had nailed Him to that Cross: "**Father, forgive them, they know not what they do**" (Luke 23:34). Seek forgiveness. And pray for the gift of mercy to forgive those who have hurt you.

Love God and let Him love you. There is a Scriptural passage that reads, "Behold, I stand at the door and knock. If anyone hears my voice and opens the door, [then] I will enter his house and dine with him, and he with me" (Revelation 3:20). Think about this: When we sit down to eat with someone, we get to better know that person. We build a relationship. When I invited Jesus into my heart to "dine" with me,

I got to know Him and love Him better. Invite Jesus in. Spend time with Him in prayer and Scriptural and spiritual reading. Pray for guidance. Trust Him. Desire a relationship with Him with all your heart.

> *The true measure of loving God*
> *is to love Him without measure.*
>
> ~ SAINT BERNARD OF CLAIRVAUX

Stay in the present. When I invited Jesus into my heart, I receive the gift of being content, of being able to live in the present moment. When we spend our every moment with Jesus, the past is gone and the future is not even a thought. And when we live in the present moment, no matter what is going on, we know Jesus is walking with us, holding our hand, and conversing with us in our hearts.

Do not be afraid. One of my friends often says, "Do not be afraid. Everything is already all right because Jesus is here right now." The closer you get to God, the more you will trust Him. The more you trust Him, the more hope you will have. The more hope you have, the more you will be content to live in and enjoy the present moment.

Smiling makes you feel good. That's the lesson I learned in the mall that day when I really didn't feel much like smiling. I got twenty smiles for my investment. When we give something of ourselves to others, we can't help but feel better.

What I learned that day helped me through my illnesses. Even at my sickest, I was able to smile at the doctors and medical staff; and when I smiled at them, they smiled back at me, and I felt peace in my heart. Try it!

> *Whenever anything disagreeable*
> *or displeasing happens to you,*
> *remember Christ crucified and be silent.*
>
> ~ SAINT JOHN OF THE CROSS

Unpleasant things happen. Life can be hard, sometimes very painful. You may be suffering right now. But know this: God is on your side. He loves you, unconditionally loves you. You can never do anything to destroy His love. And to show you how much He loves you, He gave you His Son Jesus, the Light of the World, to hold your hand, to walk with you.

Pain and suffering are inevitable, but we can find meaning in our pain and suffering if we connect ourselves to Jesus on His Cross. Remember God's love. Remember He loves us so much He gave us His Son, who sacrificed Himself in expiation for our sins. Love and Sacrifice beget Love. Love God. In great suffering, Christ is closest to us.

You are wonderfully made. You are worthy of love. God loves you unconditionally. He wants good things for you.

God is good. On that day in Millie's front yard, I fell in love with God. And then came hope. Hope led me to joy and peace. And this is my prayer for you: That you realize how much God loves you and wants to be with you—to "dine" with you every day. That you experience the joy of loving Him and living in the present moment. That you, too, can pray: "You never go away from us, yet we have difficulty in returning to You. Come Lord, stir us up and call us back. Kindle and seize us. Be our fire and our sweetness. Let us love. Let us run....Late have I loved You, Lord...And see, You touched me and I am set on fire for Your peace."[9]

80 ◆ 03

Reflection

"All good giving and every perfect gift is from above, coming down from the Father of lights" (James 1:17).

80 ◆ 03

EVERY SUNRISE

Every sunrise is a present,
a gift from God above,
Gift wrapped with scarlet ribbons
and tied with bows of love.
Each is a new beginning,
a time to start anew,
While all the stars are sleeping,
and the rose is fresh with dew.
Each day's a new creation,
too lovely to ignore,
And we may not find a blessing
just outside our door.
We cannot keep the past,
like fireflies in a jar,
Nor journey to the future
by wishing on a star.
Every sunrise is a blessing,
a gift for just today,
Rejoice my friend, embrace it,
before it fades away!

~ Author Unknown ~

· PART FOUR ·

If your heart is at PEACE, that is from GOD.
If your heart is the least bit agitated
or uncomfortable,
then GOD is saying 'NO'.
One has to honestly listen to one's heart.
This is what I mean by listening to your heart.

~ JOAN BROWN ~

❧ ◆ ☙

REFLECTIONS:
ON THE JOURNEY

Looking back on my life, I have been so blessed. First by my mother, who taught me about God; and then by the Sisters of St. Benedict in Evansville, who kept me faithful in seeking Him by enkindling my love for Jesus in the Eucharist.

I am profoundly grateful for my precious husband. Thank you, Jerry, for all the loving support you have always given and continue to give me.

I am eternally thankful for Millie, who challenged me to seek a deeper relationship with God—a challenge that I accepted, and a challenge that was blessed when God graciously led me into deeper relationship with Him.

I am also deeply grateful for all of my dear friends who stormed heaven for me when I was ill and supported me with their love and patient kindness. Your prayers covered me with a warm blanket when I needed it most. Your love and friendship mean more to me than I can express, and I would like to thank each and every one of you from the bottom of my heart for the blessings you have given me.

I especially want to thank Brother Joel Giallanza for his spiritual guidance and Father Charlie Garza, who told me to write this book.

Lord, for the continuous sunrise of my life, for allowing me to live fully in the present moment, for giving me the gift of Jerry and our children, and the gift of yearning for You, I thank You.

Jesus for inviting me to walk my journey with You and for holding my hand every step of the way, and most of all, for carrying me when I could not take that step, I thank You. You taught me not to dwell in the past or worry about the future; You taught me to live in the present moment and trust You. You are with me every moment of my life, never have You left me, and this is such a great comfort. Thank You Jesus for giving me Your peace.

Thank You Holy Spirit for the gift of words, which I have set down here with all my love.

This is Your book. I pray it draws others ever closer to Your love.

ဆ ◆ infinity

SUNRISE PRAYER

Come Divine Will,
Come to reign in me.
With this one act,
I want to embrace my entire day
Every word, every action,
And all the people I meet.
The things I do, all my duties,
I want all to be in Your Most Holy Will.
I want to put my whole day right
From this instant in Your Most Holy Will
So that should I be distracted
Or should there be things I forget,
They may all be done in Your Will.

Amen.

CONTEMPLATIONS FOR YOUR JOURNEY

*The Lord manifests Himself to those who stop
for some time in peace and humility of heart.
If you look in murky and turbulent waters,
you cannot see the reflection of your face.
If you want to see the face of Christ,
stop and collect your thoughts in silence,
and close the door of your soul
to the noise of external things.*

~ SAINT ANTHONY OF PADUA

When my friend Millie told me that I did not know God, I set out to prove her wrong. In the process, I realized God's love for me, and I discovered Jesus "knocking on the door" of my heart. When I threw open that door and begged, "Please don't ever leave," He replied, "I will be here always if you keep the door open."

"How do I keep the door open?" I prayed.

"By conversing with me daily," was His answer.

In my daily time with Jesus, He has shown me what I need to do to live with Him. He showed me that I needed to let go of the past, and the only way to do this is to forgive. He has graciously walked with me on the road to forgiveness; and in forgiving, I have experienced a wash of healing that has given me the freedom to live in the present moment. My Sunrise!

> *I am the light of the world.*
> *Whoever follows me will not walk in darkness,*
> *but will have the light of life.*
>
> ~ JOHN 8:12

Would you like to experience the Sunrise of Jesus, the Light of the World?

What God has done for me, He will do for you. Open the door and invite Him in. He will take your hand and walk with you.

Following are contemplation questions related to this book. They are provided here for reflection as you consider your journey to a deeper relationship with our Lord who loves you so very very much.

ঙ ◆ ଓ

INVITING GOD IN

Sometimes, God speaks to us in a thought or in our hearts. Occasionally, we may hear His words in our heads. The most important thing to learn is to listen to God so you know His voice when He speaks to you.

Do you believe that God loves you?

Would you like to be filled with God's love for you? Let Him know! Then sit quietly and listen to your heart.

Reflections:

LETTING GO OF THE PAST

What big sticks and stones have hurt you?

What kinds of salve have you used to mask your pain? Were they effective?

Are you experiencing physical, emotional, or spiritual pain right now?

Is there another person with whom you can share your feelings and concerns?

If you are feeling sad and downtrodden, you might consider taking a trip to the mall just as I did. Look each person you meet in the eye and smile at them. When you go home, reflect on or write about how you feel.

What can you do to give your pain to God, to allow Him in His mercy to heal and renew your spirit?

Reflections:

The fruit of Silence is Prayer;
the fruit of Prayer is Faith;
the fruit of Faith is Love;
the fruit of Love is Service;
the fruit of Service is Peace.

~ MOTHER TERESA OF CALCUTTA

FORGIVING OTHERS

What scars are on your heart?

How have they affected the person you are today?

Do you harbor feelings of bitterness and unforgiveness?

If there are feelings of bitterness, can you write them down? (Expressing our feelings on paper can be very freeing.)

What may have happened to the people who hurt you that caused them to treat you the way they did?

Reflecting on your past hurts, how do you feel about the person(s) who caused you pain?

Do you think some of the hurts you have received from others might have been unintentional?

Did your pain bring you closer to God? Why or why not?

Forgiveness is a decision. You may want to write down those you need to forgive for past hurts.

Reflections:

I will give you a new heart,
and a new spirit I will put within you.
I will remove the heart of stone from your flesh
and give you a heart of flesh.

~ EZEKIEL 36:26

FORGIVING OURSELVES

Did your suffering cause you to react in a way that hurt yourself or someone else?

How might your actions unintentionally hurt others?

Can you seek forgiveness and forgive yourself?

Reflections:

WALKING WITH JESUS

When you are going through a difficult time, put your hand out and let Jesus hold it and feel His love for you. Although He already knows, tell Him your fears and worries; then sit quietly, listen to His response in your heart and mind, and feel the peace He wants you to have.

Often we worry about the future, and what we worry about never happens. How do you feel about what is happening in your life right now? What worries do you struggle with?

What do you fear? What power do your fears have in your life?

How do you deal with your fears and worries? Can you entrust them to God and live in the present moment with Him, or do you give your fears and concerns to Him and then continue to worry?

Have you asked God for something when you were fearful, worried, or facing a desperate situation with seemingly no answers? How did He respond?

As you reflect on your life, were there times when Jesus was with you, "holding your hand"?

Did you realize He was walking with you at the time? Can you hold out your hand and visualized Jesus holding it? How do you feel?

Consider, "He is knocking on the door of your heart every moment of every day" and then pray for a listening heart.

When a good thing happens, do you recognize God's hand in it? Can you recall a time when an angel from God may have been sent to you?

What blessings have you received from your crosses? Can you express your gratitude for the blessings you have received?

Reflections:

Don't spend your energies on things that
generate worry, anxiety, and anguish;
only one thing is necessary:
Lift up your spirit and love God.

~ SAINT PADRE PIO

Surely then you may lift up your face in innocence;
You may stand firm and unafraid.
For then you shall forget your misery,
Like water that has ebbed away you shall regard it.
Then your life shall be brighter than the noonday;
Its gloom shall become like the morning,
And you shall be secure, because there is hope.

~ JOB 11:15–18 ~

ᘂ ◆ ᘖ

ADDITIONAL RESOURCES

ONLINE

Understanding the Bible

www.usccb.org/bible/understanding-the-bible/index.cfm

Daily Reflections

www.usccb.org/bible/reflections/index.cfm

What is Prayer?

www.usccb.org/prayer-and-worship/prayers-and-devotions/prayers/what-is-prayer.cfm

"How to Listen When God is Speaking" with Father Mitch Pacwa, SJ

www.youtube.com/watch?v=NJDqlyMEMYU

"Contemplative Prayer" with Father Benedict Groeschel

www.youtube.com/watch?v=oeMheOdUjd8

BOOKS

The New American Bible, Revised Edition

http://usccb.org/bible

Facing Forgiveness by Loughlan Sofield, Carroll Juliano, and Archbishop Gregory M. Aymond

www.avemariapress.com/product/1-59471-122-4/Facing-Forgiveness

Thirsting for God by Mother Teresa of Calcutta, compiled by Angelo D. Scolozzi, M.C. III. O

www.catholiccompany.com/thirsting-god-i11929

A Simple Path by Mother Teresa of Calcutta

www.amazon.com/A-Simple-Path-Mother-Teresa/dp/0345397452

The Joy of Loving by Mother Teresa of Calcutta

www.amazon.com/The-Joy-Loving-Living-Compass/dp/0140196072

The Cloud of Unknowing translated by Mishtooni Bose

> books.google.com/books/about/The_Cloud_of_Unkn owing.html?id=VFBg1J0MQ84C

Ascent of Mount Carmel by Saint John of the Cross

> www.ccel.org/ccel/john_cross/ascent.html

Dark Night of the Soul by Saint John of the Cross

> www.ccel.org/ccel/john_cross/dark_night.html

The Joy of Full Surrender by Jean-Pierre de Caussade, revised translation by Hal M. Helms

> www.barnesandnoble.com/w/joy-of-full-surrender-jean-pierre-de-caussade/1102042958

The Practice of the Presence of God by Brother Lawrence

> http://thepracticeofthepresenceofgod.com/how-to-purchase

Notes

INTRODUCTION— First Light

[1] All Scriptural quotations in this book are from the *New American Bible, Revised Edition* [NABRE] © 2010, 1991, 1986, 1970 Confraternity of Christian Doctrine, Inc., Washington, DC.

PART ONE

CHAPTER ONE— Hard Times

[2] An accurate depiction of what life was like during the Dust Bowl can be found in *The Grapes of Wrath* by John Steinbeck, published in 1939. The movie version of this story, starring Henry Fonda and directed by John Ford, was release in 1940.

CHAPTER SEVEN— THE THIRD STONE

[3] Shakespeare, William. *The Merchant of Venice* (late 1590s), Act IV, scene 1, line 184.

PART TWO

CHAPTER EIGHT—A NEW DAWN

[4] Augustine of Hippo. (397) 2009. "Book X." *The Confessions*. Translated by Henry Chadwick. Oxford: Oxford World Classics.

CHAPTER TEN—A FLOOD OF MEMORIES

[5] Roosevelt, Franklin D. "Prayer on D-Day" (June 6, 1944). Online by Gerhard Peters and John T. Woolley, The American Presidency Project. http://www.presidency.ucsb.edu/ws/?pid=16515

CHAPTER TWELVE—OUT OF DIFFICULTIES

[6] Luke 14:27 (NABRE).
[7] Psalms 73:23, Isaiah 41:13 (NABRE).

PART THREE

CHAPTER EIGHTEEN—THE UNEXPECTED

[8] This is a reference to the novel, *The Man in the Iron Mask* by Alexandre Dumas.

CHAPTER TWENTY-THREE—EVERY PERFECT GIFT

[9] Augustine of Hippo. (397) 2009. "Book X." *The Confessions*. Translated by Henry Chadwick. Oxford: Oxford World Classics.